Living Between the Lines:

Powerful Mind Training for Overcoming Anxiety & Depression

By: Lauren Duroy, DNP, APRN, FNP-C

Foreword

Hello Fear.

I am done playing defense.

Bring it.

Anxiety and depression are real and tangible problems. But, the thoughts they produce are deceptive, faulty, little gremlins. These thoughts are wrapped up in partial truth. They disguise themselves as reality and trick you into believing them. They are sneaky and manipulative, but rather convincing. You never even think twice to second–guess their inaccuracy, which is how they thrive so well in your mind. It feels like you are constantly living between the lines of "I'm okay" to, "How do I ever get through this?" You can feel like every thing is okay, until you realize you having read the fine print.

But, there is good news. Once you learn how to read between the lines of anxiety and depression,, you can break free of them. You are at war with these nasty little gremlins and the way you defeat them in the same way you defeat any enemy: find their weaknesses and attack them. When you're afraid of failing, when you're afraid of losing, when you are anxious about performing well; when you think you are not enough; don't hide...

Go after those fears.

Attack them.

Defeat them.

Here is the beauty of learning the secrets to anxiety and depression. You start to dissect out their lies, like a science project. You discover and destroy the root of where they were planted in your life, and you watch them shrivel up and die.

You are no longer reactive.

You are active.

You are not overcome.

You overcome.

Throughout this book, I challenge you to pray dangerously. Pray that your creator will send you to accomplish amazing things. Anxiety and depression are complicated and hard. But, while being a part of the extraordinary is rarely easy, it is always worth it. The reward of what you will learn and gain into your own insight will be priceless. If you refocus your energy, there is power in knowing that what is difficult now, can be used for incredible power later. I have seen it happen in my office and in my own life which is why I am so excited to be sharing with you these gems to unlock your Powerful Mind. The first thing I want you to identify, is that you are separate from your anxiety or depression.

They define you no more than hypertension can define a patient. They may modify the way you take care of yourself. They may present with a separate set of challenges. But, they do not define you. The secret to renouncing their power is to identify the patterns and tricks that they pace on you. Then, like a cockroach, when the lights are flipped on, they scatter.

They try to give us rules and thoughts to live by, but these are inaccurate. When you discover the real meaning and root cause of these thoughts, you begin to read between their lines and are no longer forced to live between their lines. I will teach you how to do this by discovering what your thoughts and feelings really mean, through an effective treatment known as Cognitive Behavioral Therapy (CBT). Unfortunately, CBT often requires either expensive therapy sessions or reading a long book. This book introduces a new approach That allows you to implement without either. It simplifies the most effective tools in CBT, to help you get started on the road to recovery as quickly and easily as possible.

It is recommended to read the sections in order. Many of the lessons build upon one another. However, you may effectively skip directly to some, such as dealing with procrastination. Use the "Tool Box" pages in the back of this book to quickly reference your most essential "Ah ha!"'moments, during challenging times. This book was written with discretion and simplicity in mind. The cover is generic with vague description and small, so you can keep it with you at all times and use it on the go, even in public

Our first chapter briefly explores simple changes that will decrease your overall anxiety and allow you to live more uplifted. Shrek's friend, Donkey, was spot on. We are like onions. (If this reference loses you, it Is from Shrek, a children's movie about an Ogre and his friend, Donkey. The movie is quite hilarious and rather insightful. Like onions, we have many layers and each one is important. However, these many layers mean we can't search for a quick fix. We have to look at the big picture. Luckily, you are holding a reference on how to start peeling back the layers.

On a final note, this book offers some Christian perspective. If you are currently are not a follower of Jesus, this book will still apply to you. If you decide upon reading this book, you want to become one, I recommend you speak with a spiritual leader you trust; just as I recommend seeing a medical provider for the implementation of any medical advice. While Gods' grace is available to absolutely everyone, there are sometimes steps, such as repentance, that may need to be taken in

order for us to receive His grace. Evaluating this need is beyond the scope of this book.

Now let's get started!!

The secret is not to stay in a hurry getting to

where you are going, but to remember

why you don't want to go back

to where you came from.

–Dr. Lauren, DNP, APRN

Table of Contents

Chapter 1 : General Tips for Decreasing Stress...9

Chapter 2: Powerful Mind Training & Learning the Tricks of Anxiety and

       Depression..16

Chapter 3: Finding Your True Feelings & Identity Priorities...............................33

Chapter 4: Overcoming Perfectionism & Fear....................................…..........….43

Chapter 5: But, "THEY" made me mad!...…..........50

Chapter 6: Deceptive Rules & Limiting Beliefs......................……….................…58

Chapter 7: Squashing NATs...67

Chapter 8: Letting Go (of Being Wronged)..…...........…72

Chapter 9: Be a Kid In a Candy Store.......………................................…..........…79

Chapter 10: Move the Mountain: Procrastination ...……………….................…..86

Chapter 11: Closing Words………..…..............…92

Personal Toolbox..............................,.......…..95

Background

I would like to give you some background as to why I wrote this book. I practice

family medicine in the state of Oklahoma. I have always believed that mental health is

the single most important aspect of our lives. However, treatment is often complex

and remission of anxiety and depression are difficult to obtain. In all honesty, my

initial plan after I started practicing on my own was to refer my complex patients to a

psychiatrist. As luck would have it, that did not turn out to be feasible.

My region happens to receive some of the lowest funding available to mental

health in our nation. Additionally, it is a part of the severe mental health shortage.

Therefore, I had to treat these individuals on my own. Frustrated with the lack of

support, a fire was lit underneath me. I saw how anxiety and depression were

deteriorating the quality of life in my patients and I set out to put an end to it. I read

several books on Cognitive Behavioral Therapy (CBT) and started to put it to use in

my clinic and personal life. Initially, implementing CBT with my patients was

intimidating. It is complex and often reveals very hidden, deep, dark secrets that if not

healed when brought to the surface, can cause damage. With that said, this book is

recommended to be used in conjunction with a mental health professional who is

trained in helping you accurately assess some of the issues you will uncover. CBT can

be a very effective part of anyone's treatment plan and I am thrilled to be sharing with

you its basic functions.

I then saw firsthand how powerful it is. Unfortunately, implementing this

approach via traditional methods requires a lot of reading and/or time spent in long sessions. Most individuals do not feel they can commit to that. Furthermore, office appointments do not allot the time needed to fully implement such interventions. Therefore, I had additionally had to find a way to simplify it. I went back to my office, determined to figure out a way that I could get CBT to my patients in a quick and effective way and Living Between the Lines was created. I am now sharing this with you.

Chapter 1:

General Tips for

Decreasing Stress

The Secret to Happiness

is to let situations be as they are,

not how we feel they should be.

1. Do the math. It's easy to blame the proverbial "straw" that broke the donkey's back. But, often not much attention is given to the little things that add up to a big deal. This is unfortunate because they tend to be what we have the most control over. Focus inward and take note of what little things irritate or upset you. Then, prevent them from occurring or identify why they bother you and change your thoughts about them (more on how to do that later). This may be uncomfortable clothing, tedious rituals, awkwardly placed utensils, clutter in your workplace, or unnecessarily micromanaging others.

2. Simplify your life. Does your stress start with picking out what to wear in the mornings? Then, decrease your options and donate the rest. Do you stress about dinner? Find a meal plan online and stick to it. Use delivery services for easy shopping. We easily make tens of thousands of decisions a day. More is not better; it adds to us being overwhelmed and easily triggers anxiety and depression. Make a rule to always choose from one of the first three options and move on with your life.

On the same note as your environment, try to keep it uplifting. Organize your areas so it is not anxiety provoking and it aesthetically keeps you uplifted. Companies spend millions of dollars a year on packaging because we know the science behind how visual details evoke certain emotions (Grenny, et al 2014). Your personal environment is no different. We are visual creatures, embrace that.

3. Be present. These days are chalked full of "doing". Multitasking is as much a way of life, as a badge of honor, but it's overwhelming. Many cultures place a high value on meditation, and for good reason. It is proven to increase longevity and overall health (Bhargava, 2016). Incorporate daily meditation and mental relaxation into your daily routine. This can be done formally with traditional meditation or by just focusing on one simple thing. For example, stop working while eating lunch. Focus only on the taste and nourishment it provides your body. Clear your mind and dedicate time to reflect on your values and what you are thankful for.

4. Disconnect to reconnect. In doing this you can once again focus on the things that matter without feeling like they are an annoyance. Our daily lives are jam-packed with pop-ups, reminders, and advertisements. All 100% designed to "get you going". Whether it's getting you excited to buy something or open a new app, notifications produce (often) unnecessary stimulation, add to our to-do list, and easily lead to overload. Don't get so wrapped up in the virtual world and ancillary details, that your real-world becomes an annoyance.

5. Get your sleep. Less than 5 hours of sleep a night is not generally safe and can severely exacerbate symptoms of depression and anxiety (Brauser, 2017). Make sleep a priority. If you struggle with insomnia, seek help. CBT can also treat insomnia. My personal favorite trick for falling asleep is to read hard to focus on material. I have to be careful for it to not be too interesting or even that can keep me awake. Other tips for sleep include making sure your phone is changed from blue light to yellow light settings, no phone or TV use at night, dimming the lights and only using warm lights at night, keeping the same schedule and avoiding carbohydrates late at night.

6. Treat yourself right. Make time for yourself. If you're a mom or dad who works yourself to the core for others, identify the harm you are doing for everyone and stop it. In an airplane, the parent puts the mask on himself or herself before helping their children. Why? Because the parent won't do anyone any good passed out on the floor. You need oxygen and room to breathe the same as everyone else.

7. Cut the crap. Americans are pumped full of chemicals known to cause depressed and anxious moods (as well as substances that haven't even been studied). Chemicals like MSG, food coloring and added sugars mess with our hormones and are proven to have side effects that exacerbate anxiety and depression (MacReady, 2019). Adopt a clean diet and feel the benefits.

8. Get a move on. Exercise is a natural and powerful way to boost hormones that decrease the occurrence of anxiety and depression, while increasing motivation, self-worth, and energy (Piedmont Health Care, 2018).

9. When you can't stand, kneel. With that said, you do not have to be Christian to learn from this book. It is simply my experience that a truly selfless, Christian approach is the most rewarding one. That is not to say that we do not fall from grace from time to time. But, the Bible is called the Living Word for virtuous reasons. It speaks across generations and cultures. For centuries God has led people from despair and changed lives like no one else ever could. The purpose, meaning, and sheer strength that God gives us, can be the most powerful tool available to you. If you are new to the word, I recommend getting a New International Version (NIV) with interpretations in the margins and an index for key discussions on topics such as rejection, anger, anxiety, or sadness to deepen your study. Remember though, that powerful does not mean easy. It just means worth it. Those who strive to be in oneness with the world, receive His mercy and grace. If you have given yourself to the Lord and are ready to live for the higher purpose for all,   almost everything we feel anxious or depressed over ceases to have power. When we live 'horizontally' we compare ourselves to others on invisible scales and end up defeated. When we live 'vertically', we look towards Him for value in our lives and we are launched into meaningful living beyond our visual horizons (Marsh, 2018).

10. Work smarter, not harder! These days there is almost always a better, easier, cheaper way to do anything. Get on the Internet and research life-hacks for daily hang-ups. You can also check out my Time-Management Course for getting more done in less time.

11. Don't *practice* your anxiety or depression. Many people pretend to be okay in public, then at home the rages or moping sessions reign. Anxiety and depression can be practiced and perfected like any other skill. Even when no one is watching you are building muscle memory for your body to react upon. The amygdala in your brain learns your fears and correlates them to your surroundings (Potter-Efron, 2007). The more you tell it to react, the more it will influence your perception and reactions, and the better it will get at doing so (Knaus, 2014). Stress is a primitive instinct that allows us to run from danger. The faster we react the quicker we can possibly get away from physical danger. However, if this instinct is "over developed" it can become hypersensitive to triggers. This means that your "fight or flight" will get good at kicking in for even the small things.

12. **Obtain an accurate mindset.** Have you ever heard the saying, "Fear is a liar"? Well, it's true. Anxiety and fear are often nothing more than our false interpretation of current circumstances (Potter-Efron, 2007). Even better put: it is False Evidence Appearing Real. As anxiety takes over, the analytic, thinking part of our brain shuts down and the quick reaction part takes over. This part of our brain is important in life or death circumstances. It is still needed today, though less often than the days when animals such as lions could more easily prey on us. Most of us no longer have lions to fear. Instead, we have due dates, finances, and the like. Our mind is screaming, "Lion! Lion!", when in fact there is no lion (Potter-Efron, 2007). However, we still react as if there is. Remind yourself there is no lion. You will not be eaten alive. That is what this powerful mindset training will help you to develop.

13. **Let go of standards that DO NOT exist.** When we compare ourselves to those around us we are using fake standards. Common examples of this include being "pretty", "smart", "funny", etc. Let me give an example. My entire childhood I believed my name was ugly. When I would see it, I would cringe inside. Then one day I looked down and was excited to see my name, it was pretty to me for some reason. Why did it all of a sudden look pretty to me?

Without realizing it, I had been associating my name with how I felt about myself. My perception of my name being pretty or ugly, never had anything to do with having the name itself. The person associated with my name was finally someone who I liked. I could now see that my name was pretty too. But, the point is that ALL names are beautiful. The standard of a "prettier name…figure…anything" DOES NOT exist.

What does exist is individuality and that is what is beautiful. The world needs your individual look, style, and past. It brings diversity and beauty. If we were all the same or even similar there wouldn't be much that we could be interested in. You were created an original for good reason; don't try to die a copy! Look at yourself from the perspective that your Father looks at you, and you will see your beauty. *…That of your inner self, the unfading beauty of a gentle and quiet spirit, which is of great worth in God's sight.* (1 Peter 3:4)

Now that we have a basic foundation for success, let's dive right into the good stuff! Cognitive Behavioral Therapy (CBT) begins with identifying the illusions of mental illness. They are what keep anxiety and depression burning within us. They are tricky. It is easy to believe them. However, once we know what they are and how to read between their crooked lines, we see the root of their fallacy and can disprove and renounce them. It is then that we start to suffocate out anxiety and depression like a roaring fire that runs out of oxygen.

One final note, before we begin, is that this book does offer some Christian perspective. If you are currently not a follower of Jesus and decide upon reading this book, that you want to become one, I recommend speaking with a spiritual leader you trust. Just as the implementation of any medical advice should be discussed with your health care provider, so should your Christian walk be with a spiritual leader. While God's' grace is available to everyone, there are sometimes steps that may need to be taken in order for you to receive His grace. Evaluating this need is beyond the scope of this book.

Chapter 2:

Powerful Mind Training

& Learning The Tricks

of Anxiety & Depression

Doubt Kills More

Dreams than

failure ever will.

This chapter is a large basis for what we will be using on our journey to peace. You will refer back to this often. I would recommend tagging this chapter. Depression and anxiety promote and maintain negative perceptions through predictable mechanisms. We will call them tricks. They are outlined in the following pages and identifying them is the first step to overcoming anxiety and depression. They are not thought on purpose but are very convincing. They work similarly to the "magic" tricks performed by magicians (Burns, 2009). They can be thought of as symptoms of depression and anxiety; the same way headaches are potential symptoms of high blood pressure. They become a trap for negative mood swings and cloud rational thinking. Fortunately, once identified they become easy to disprove and therefore occur less often, and eventually stop altogether. Consider whether you have thoughts that fall into any of the next categories. You may need to confide in a close friend, relative, or health care provider to help you make the connections. The following pages describe these 11 common tricks of anxiety and depression.

Trick 1: Absolute Thinking

Absolute Thinking is seeing everything as only one way, typically badly, once one thing goes wrong (Ostell & Oakland, 2001). For example, catching a red light and thinking, "This *always* happens to me!" It is very unlikely that you *always* catch red lights. However, green lights are not anxiety-provoking, and therefore stand out less. Red lights may *seem* to occur more often. This lends us to focus on the bad more. Even if it is frequent, but not literally "always", thinking such thoughts is anxiety provoking and can easily spin us out of control.

Overgeneralizations are very common in Absolute Thinking. They are your first cue that we may need to change the thoughts we are telling ourselves. It uses inaccurate, absolute thinking such as "always, "never", "everything" or "all" bad (Knaus, 2014). Be precise in your wording. Completely remove absolutes from your dialect. Stop saying, "This always happens to me!" or "He always does this!" These statements are most likely inaccurate anyhow and lead to unreasonable thinking and unnecessary anger. Have you ever been told "You always do blank!" by a loved one in a fight? It is a very common way for individuals to lash out at others as well as themselves. It hurts, doesn't it? You know that it is inaccurate and therefore it makes you even madder. Avoid doing this to yourself, as well as to others. Keep your perspective as accurate as possible so your molehill doesn't turn into a mountain.

Here is what to do to remove this unwarranted evil from your life:

1. Commit to training your mind to catch the little gems in life, that you are thankful for. Focus and write down the times that you didn't catch the proverbial red lights (or other anxiety provoking events). Regularly remind yourself of the times you thought your day would go horrible it didn't! Focus on the wins, not the losses and you will attract more wins!

2. Start looking for the positive and you will begin to find it.

3. Remove absolute wording from your vocabulary. Stop saying "always", "never", "everyone", etc.

What is something that is easy to overgeneralize about?

How are these thoughts not entirely (or at all) true?

Write down positive truths that disprove your negative thoughts. Reflect back on these regularly.

Trick 2: All or Nothing Thinking

This is applying overgeneralizations to personal qualities (Rnic, Dozois, Martin, 2016). For example, believing you're a failure because you performed poorly in one situation or area. People cannot be all bad, all good, all smart, all dumb, so on and so on. We are simply too complex for any of this to be true. An example is, "I lost the deal. I am a failure." Let's analyze this. What's the percentage of failures that makes someone a failure? Is it 30%...50%...70%? What about someone who invented dozens of inventions and lost money on every single one, except the last one. The last one made them a millionaire. Are they a failure? They "failed" almost every time, after all! Failure is not defined by one event or even several events. As long as you haven't given up on yourself, you cannot be a failure, because the game is simply not over! Write down some personal examples of All or Nothing Thinking.

How are these thoughts inaccurate? What additional qualities do you have that do not fit these negative labels?

What else do you do well?

Trick 3: Disqualifying the Positive

Disqualifying the Positive is not taking credit for good accomplishments or qualities (Rnic, Dozois, Martin, 2016). For example, doing something good and calling it "dumb luck" or rejecting a compliment because it isn't "the real you" or "they were just being nice". Think about this logically. The odds of luck repeating itself are much lower than the odds of you taking control and owning it! Meaningful action beats luck, statistically speaking, every time. You killed it; so own it! If something was a challenge for you, embrace the growth you gained from it, but still, appreciate that you rocked its world while you could!

What positive qualities about yourself do you disqualify?

How can you start identifying your good qualities?

What positive qualities about yourself do you disqualify?

How can you start identifying your good qualities?

Who does it benefit to rob yourself of a job well done?

What positive things have you done that originally appeared negative or mediocre?

Trick 4: False Prophecies

False Prophecies involve assuming the worst before the facts are known. There are two types. The first is "mind-reading" (Burns, 2016). For example, thinking someone avoided eye contact with you and rashly concluding they do not like you. This is "mind-reading", and you do not have the power to do it (despite what your emotions tell you). Maybe the other person was just in deep thought and they weren't avoiding you at all. The second type of False Prophecy is fortune-telling. It is when you predict something bad will come of a situation before it occurs. We also do not have the power to do this, not at least without a crystal ball (Burns, 2016). An example of this is, assuming your entire day will go awfully because it started off by spilling coffee on your shirt.

False Prophecies are damaging because they get us worked up well before we even know whether we have something to be worked up about. Then when something is worth getting worked up about, we are already so wound up, it gets to us so bad we can't cope.

Stop and think, "Do I actually *know* this is going to happen or am I *assuming* it will?" Start to take notice of the times you just "knew" something was going to go wrong and it didn't. Write down these examples in the space below, as they happen. These will prove to you how often False Prophecies occur and serve as a reminder for you in the future to not "count your chickens before they hatch."

What "mind-reading" have you done in the past that turned out to be inaccurate?

What "fortune telling" have you assumed would be bad and turned out okay?

Use these examples to remind yourself of how things can easily work out when they seem impossible or unsolvable. Nothing is impossible. Even the word itself reads "I'm Possible."

Trick 5. Emotional reasoning

Using emotions to form facts or opinions. For example, feeling like a loser, therefore viewing yourself as such. Or feeling that a chore or event will be dreadful, therefore expecting it to be before ever trying.

A great objective example of this is the false "feeling" of going backward. Have you ever parked your car at the same exact time that the car next to you was pulling out? It gives you this wild feeling of being catapulted forward. You react by slamming on the breaks even harder. Then you realize what was going on. You relax and may even laugh. But man, that experience really felt real! A similar experience is being in an optical illusion fun-house where you feel like you are walking crooked and everything is actually flat. It *feels* real, but only because you can't let go of your perception of how things *should be*. Feelings are not always reliable. There are times when we need to step back and look at our emotions objectively. Emotions are strong and they can apply a real effect on us, but that does not mean that we should always lead with them. When your emotions are telling you something that is counterproductive for your own health and well-being, it is time to start using cognitive behavioral therapy.

Do you do any emotional reasoning?

What causes these thoughts? Fear? Insecurity?

What proof is there that these feelings are true?

How are they inaccurate?

Does it benefit you to believe these things?

How can you change this thinking?

Trick 6: Should-of, Could-of,

and Would-of Thinking

(SOCOWO Thinking)

We will abbreviate this as "SOCOWO Thinking". SOCOWO Thinking tends to come in the form of   lamenting over the past. This occurs in two main themes:

1) *Not acting or reacting the right way.* For example, "I shouldn't have eaten that cake", or

2) *Being wronged by someone:* For example, "they shouldn't have done that to me!"

What do you lament over?

How has worrying helped?

If you are human (or the other individual is), and humans are expected to make mistakes, could accidents be expected and accepted?

They can be, especially if the best attempt was made, under the circumstances given.

How can you help make it right?

How can you learn and grow from it, or turn it into a positive outcome?

Get rid of the "Should-of, Could-of, Would-of" by accurately restructuring your thoughts:

Step 1: *Get it Right.* This is a modified version from "Feeling Good" by Dr. Burns. Which is a great additional read. Identify why it *should* have occurred that way. Just as cars break down, humans mess up. Identify why the slip-up occurred. For example, if a lack of preparation leads to eating fast food, then it makes sense you slipped up on your diet. Accept that you are human and forage on! Just as important, screen the situation for inaccurately applying the wrong cause with the wrong outcome. For example, it is inaccurate to blame yourself for a loved one wrecking after they left your home. Not allowing people to leave your house does not prevent wrecks. Letting people leave does not cause wrecks.

Step 2: *Word it Right.* Exchange "Should of", "Could of", "Would of" for a more positive, accurate phrase. For example, instead of saying, "I shouldn't have eaten that burger", say, "Next time I will eat healthier" or "It would have been best to not eat the burger. But, I was not prepared, hungry, and rushed. Good or not, there was a reason why I should have done what I did."

Step 3: *Find the Right:* Identify any positive outcomes. Every mistake provides opportunity, knowledge, and a drive to do better next time. This is good. We learn from mistakes and this prevents them from reoccurring in the future. Be thankful for the lessons learned or for what did not go as wrong as it could have. For example, the feeling of guilt from eating unhealthy food represents determination. Be thankful for your determination and for the lesson on preparation. Feeling guilty proves you are a good person. Everyone messes up, but only good people feel bad when they do. Be glad for your conscience.

Use the following pages to journey and practice getting rid of the "SOCOWO" thinking.

Should-of, Could-of, Would-of # 1:

What happened?

Step 1: Get it Right:

Why does it make sense it happened that way?

Are there any inaccurate causes and effects being applied?

Step 2: Word it Right

It would have been better if________________

Next time________________________________

Step 3: Find the Right:

Lessons Learned:

Opportunity for improvement:

Positive meanings for our feelings:

Shoulda', Coulda', Woulda' Thought # 2:

What happened:

Step 1: Get it Right:

Why does it make sense it happened that way?

Are there any inaccurate causes and effects being applied?

Step 2: Word it Right

It would have been better if________________

Next time_______________________________

<u>Step</u> <u>3:</u> <u>Find</u> <u>the</u> <u>Right:</u>

Lessons Learned:

Opportunity for improvement:

Positive meanings for our feelings:

Trick #7: Negative Filter

Using a negative filter forces you to see only the bad, even in good situations (Strosahl & Robinson, 2017). For example, someone cooks you a nice dinner, but it was not what you wanted. Instead of feeling grateful, you get upset because you feel obligated to eat it and you fail to notice the care and love that was put into it. Having a negative filter is like using a filter on your pictures online. It changes the way things look and highlights the same feature on everything you look at, no matter what the original looks like. A negative filter on life becomes a habit. It becomes reality and your happiness is hijacked. The opposite is what they mean by, "Seeing the world through a rose-colored lens". The eyes will see what the mind perceives.

A negative past can also put our mind into a negative "autopilot." When this happens, we start focusing on negative details and therefore expecting negative outcomes. This leads us to believe more negative than positive occurs. Thinking in this manner locks up your mind and spirit in a never-ending battle of self-defeat. We start to feel overwhelmed, overcome, and overused. Then it flows over into our life on a regular basis. It's as if it is the proverbial "last straw" every time something goes wrong. Chapter 10 goes into more depth with this in helping you change your perspective. Remember: D*on't breathe so much life into your past, that it suffocates your future.*

What have you used negative filters for in the past?

What were the positive outcomes for each of them that you did not recognize?

How can you start seeing the positive in the future sooner?

Trick #8: Magnification

Magnification is blowing situations out of proportion. For example, losing sleep over assuming you offended your boss. Starting to believe that you will never have a good relationship with them any longer and work will become miserable. Then, your scores at work will drop and you won't get the raise you need and your kids might not get to go to college. When you ask them about it the next day, you find they were never offended. All over one bad moment. This is magnification.

What have you excessively worried about, just to realize it was not a big deal?

Instead of worrying, simply write out the facts. Do not use assumptions, opinions, or feelings. Do you have proof this is a big deal?

What information is missing for you to be able to prove your worries?

Is it possible you are using magnification?

*After identifying a pattern of this recurring, it becomes easier to see that the worst-case scenario is not as likely. Each time you begin to worry, remember that the alarm is more often a false alarm. Use the following pages to help you see this more

clearly.

De-Magnifying

What is a worry of yours? (Example: *I don't feel liked by my boss.*)

Why are you afraid this is true? What would this mean? (Example: *I'm not likable.*)

What if this were true, why would it be a big deal? (Example: *I will not be favored at

work.)*

How do you know it is not a big deal? *(My boss cannot legally discriminate.)*

Which of the 11 Tricks are you applying in order to make this worry true?

(Example: *I am afraid I am not likable, but the people who know me well DO like me.

Therefore, I deep down know that is not true. My boss did not say he doesn't like me;

this is an assumption. That is mind-reading. Maybe I will talk to him.)* Worse comes

to worst, if your fears are true, how can you make it a better situation? (Example: I

will continue to do the best I can. Maybe I can find a way to make amends.)

De-Magnifying: Second Worry:

Why are you afraid this is true? What would this mean?

What facts do you have that it is a big deal?

How do you know it is not a big deal?

Which of the 11 Tricks are you applying in order to make this worry true? Are you assuming someone's feeling or fortune-telling?

Worse comes to worst: If your fears are true, how can you make it a better situation?

Trick #9 Minimization:

This is accomplishing something good and classifying it as "not a big deal". This may be rooted in self-doubt. An example would be receiving praise for a job well done and saying, "they're just being nice".

What have you minimized in the past?

Has anyone ever pointed out that you don't take enough credit or are too hard on yourself?

What were you minimizing?

Why were you minimizing?

When you minimize your achievements it may be that you are being too hard on yourself and not the work itself. Instead, try to pretend it was someone else who did the work. If someone else did that work, would you still look negatively upon it?

Does it still seem to be "no big deal"?

Trick #10: Labeling:

Labeling is calling yourself something other than your name, such as dumb, lazy, or ugly. Labeling is as disruptive as it is inaccurate. No one quality can accurately label you and it is a form of shaming, which we will learn later is massively destructive. For example, you may not know a particular subject well. However, there are ones that you do know well. Therefore, you cannot *be* dumb. Additionally, if depression had anything to do with being defective, then those who treated their depression would still feel like "losers" or "failures" even after remission. This is simply not what happens. When the depression resolves, the affected person becomes productive, full of life, and eliminates negative labels.

What labeling do you do?

How is it inaccurate?

What are more positive and accurate descriptions?

Trick #11: Personalization

Personalization is inaccurately taking credit for negative outcomes by mistaking your influence or involvement in a situation, for having control over it (Burns, 2016). For example, a mother carries guilt for her child failing a class. While she is influential on her child's development (being responsible *to* her children), the child ultimately makes his or her own decisions (not responsible *for* the child's decisions). Another way that personalization occurs is through self-blame for something that was done to you. It is common for victims of abuse to apply personalization to their assault. They worry over thoughts such as, "If I would have done things differently, it wouldn't have happened to me." Or "I should have known better to better protect myself." They feel guilt for something that they did not cause and may even think that if they were a 'better' person, their abuser wouldn't have done what they did. These are all examples of applying what someone is involved in for what they have influence over. Separating out the difference between these two things can be difficult and is commonly done.

What have you influenced or were only involved in, but did not have control over, that you blame yourself for?

Ask yourself whether you actions similar to your involvement with the situation logically causes the outcome that occurred? For example, if Person A dresses, acts, or thinks a certain way, and Person B sees or hears this, is Person B forced to act beyond their own control? Could those actions of Person A automatically cause

Person B to assault Person A? The answer is no. Assault happens to people no matter how the victim is dressed or acts. Furthermore, tons of people dress, act, and react negatively every day without getting assaulted.

Ask yourself, "Does what I did always result in the outcome that occurred?" For example, do children who perform well always come from very involved and smart parents? The answer is no. While we try to make life easier for our children, and we are responsible too them, they still have free will. We can only control our own actions. The saying you can lead a horse to water, but you can't make it drink is never truer than now.

How can you apply this wisdom to see the difference in the future?

Chapter 3:

Finding Your True Feelings

and Identity Priorities

Everything happens for a reason,

discovering <u>why</u> is where

the transformation happens.

This section is about identifying how and why your depression or anxiety occurs. Write your answers in the first column while you are feeling your worst. Reflect back on these answers when you feel better and see if you still agree. If you don't, use it as a reminder that your depression/anxiety is causing irrational thinking. Negative feelings are often not about what we react to. Learning the truth can help you gain control.

It is important to understand that anger, depression, anxiousness, and sadness *are not the "feelings"* we need to identify; they are the *results* of our feelings. Workable feelings that we are looking for here answer questions like, "I feel like a ______", or "I am afraid I am a ______". They are often rooted in

1) personal responsibility (providing for the family, doing your job, etc.)

2) accomplishment (being powerful versus weak),

3) morality (feeling like a bad person), or

4) feelings of acceptance.

Feelings of acceptance must be further examined to find the description of self because they are based on others' actions (you would be accepted if you had the choice). You must ask, "What does it say about me that I am not accepted/loved?" or "*Why* is that important to me?"

I also want you to take care that you do not jump to the first thing you think of. That is why asking "WHY is this important" or "What that means ABOUT ME", is crucial. More often than not our first thought is not the real issue at hand. For example, you may initially be upset being left out of a group event. You may identify that as being wronged and that is why you say you are mad. When in fact, when you ask what does that mean ABOUT me, you may find a deeply rooted belief or fear that you may not actually be likable or lovable. If this occurs, go back to Chapter 1 and explore what tricks of anxiety and depression you are implementing to make that statement true. Rework the story that you are telling yourself. Every new thought builds a new synapse and the more you practice your powerful & positive synapses, the more your brain will being to see the positive and default to happiness and true confidence.

What are the most common feelings that you experience?

How does this give insight to your values or insecurities?

Are you being too hard on yourself? What tricks of anxiety or depression did you reveal?

Let's take a moment to identify your core beliefs. I want you to know upon taking this quiz, there is no right or wrong answer. Do not answer based upon how you would prefer to feel or what you think to know the better answer is. Answer based upon how to prioritize life and living. Base your answers upon your true, real, raw and vulnerable self. Either way, it is good. Besides, it is just you and the book. No one else will see this. If you give false testimony to yourself, you simply cannot grow & will not benefit from this very important exercise.

Now, take a moment to answer "yes", "maybe", or "no" the following questions.

1. Is being loved a necessary part of happiness?

2. If someone states they do not like you or something you did, could that ruin your day?

3. If you did not do well on a task, or respond poorly to a situation, could it emotionally cripple you?

4. If you were asked to speak in front of a group, over a topic you know well, would you decline?

5. Are you comfortable eating alone in a restaurant?

6. Is it upsetting to not get what you feel you deserve?

7. Is a job only worth doing, if you can do it alone?

8. Do you avoid asking for, or even decline, help from others?

9. Does time/being late stress you out?

Discovering Your Identity Priorities (IPs)

Anger, anxiety, & depression are rooted in misconceptions surrounding Identity Priorities, or IPs, that we often don't realize we have (de Graff, et al., 2009). Discovering your IPs will give you insight to why you have the feelings you do that you identified above. Common categories of IPs are listed below. Identify yours by reflecting on your answers from the previous page. A "yes" likely indicates imbalanced IPs relative to that category. A "maybe" indicates this is a category worth investigating. A "No" likely means you have a healthy perception of it. For example, if you answered yes to question 1 on the previous page, you should evaluate whether you place too much value on "needing" to be loved by others. While it is natural and important to have a need for love and acceptance, it is not generally healthy to *need* others' love to make you complete.

On the reverse side of that, if you feel yourself pulling away from wanting others loves too much, it may in fact mean that you are hiding a deep desire to be loved but an even stronger fear of being vulnerable. Again, be honest with yourself. Something else to consider is if you strongly reject one of the categories, that in itself might be a red flag for a imbalanced IP on the category opposite. For example, if you strongly reject Question 1, you may have too much emphasis for autonomy or a fear of being weak. Be sure to make those connections and identify any trends you see.

Question 1: Excessive need to be loved

Question 2: Needing others approval

Question 3: Need for perfectionism

Questions 4 and 5: Possible insecurity

Question 6: Sense of entitlement

Question 7: Excessive need for autonomy

Question 8: Fear of being weak

Question 9: Fear of death (running out of/wasting time)

IPs' cause semi-predictable emotions and feelings (Bernbau, et al., 1995). Knowing which ones match which IPs', can help you identify the root of your grief. Below are some examples. They may differ from person to person. Relevant feelings may be past or present.

1. A need for love: Often associated with feelings of being lonely, unloved, incomplete, or defective. You may find yourself "putting up" with more for a fear of losing someone.

2. Need for approval: Feeling like a "bad" person, incompetent, or uncomfortable in public and only proud when others first approve. Or feeling your worst when criticized.

3. Perfectionism: Feeling incompetent, rejected, unsatisfied, or never enough. You may often find yourself caught in tedious cycles.

4. Insecurity: Feeling unworthy, dirty, or disgusting. Such feelings may stem from a history of hiding personal secrets.

5. Sense of entitlement: You may notice trends of predictable irritability or dissatisfaction with others or an obsession with fairness. Maybe you often feel the need to justify others' wrongdoing.

6. Need for autonomy: Feeling distrust towards others, rejected, insecure, or needing control. May be associated with a history of chaos as a child and thus trying to desperately keep control. You may be trapped in a belief that joy comes from the outside.

7. Fear of being weak: Feeling inferior, incompetent, or threatened by others knowing how you do things. May be related to feelings of insecurity or a history of being influenced to believe you are inferior.

8. Fear of death: Stress about time-lines or excessive concern for always making the most of something. Worrying that experiences are never enough.

The following pages carry a brief discussion on overcoming unbalanced IPs. It is by no means an exhaustive study. IPs relate to certain emotions and feelings. Knowing which ones match certain IPs, can help you identify the root of your grief and which IPs you carry. Below are *examples*, but may differ from person to person. Relevant feelings may be past or presently felt.

Obtaining Healthy & Balanced IPs

Childhood experiences often trigger IPs. Consider these questions as you continue your journey to peace. Do you have a history of abuse, trauma, or rejection that subconsciously leads you to feel inferior, imperfect, or weak? Did you hide things from friends that may have left you feeling "dirty" or "wrong"? While, it can be difficult to reveal these experiences, it can also be liberating. However, you must remember them from the context of debunking any tricks of anxiety or depression that may slip into your mind. These experiences were likely out of your control and do not reflect upon you as a person. No one is completely good or bad. Remind yourself of your good qualities and be okay with the fact that you will work on others. Everyone in this world is a work in progress.

1. **On Needing Love**: Remind yourself of all the things done in the enjoyment that do not require other people. Find a hobby that you enjoy doing alone and reflect on the gratification you receive from it (painting, reading, poetry, volunteering, etc.) A need for love suggests a lack of personal appreciation or confidence. Find and cherish what makes you a great person. You offer the world something no one else has. It is a universal law that we are all unique in some way. Go further and ask yourself why

you feel the need for love from others, and identify how that is not always beneficial.
Then focus on the advantages of being autonomous. There are pros and cons to both
autonomy and dependency, striving for a healthy balance in which you place priority.

2. On Needing Approval: Anyone can be admired, but it does not make him or her a
good person. Consider Hitler. He had followers, but for the ill reason (Burns, 2009).
There are several modern-day celebrities who are not good people, but for adverse
reasons develop a following. Others' approval is not a reflection of personal value and
does not create self-worth. It may even be good to not receive their approval. Jesus
died rejected and alone. No matter your beliefs, it would be hard to argue that his life
did not matter. He powerfully influences billions of people. Others' approval is never
an accurate reflection of self-worth. Jesus' life is a strong testimony to this. You must
love yourself first.

3. Perfectionism is a never-ending battle. Even the most successful people can argue
they could do better in life. If achievement equaled worth and happiness, there would
be no rich or famous people suffering from anxiety or depression. This is obviously
not the case. Consider things that you either strive for perfectionism in or things that
cause stress. Evaluate whether the benefit is worth the stress by filling out the
following pages. Eliminate or decrease stress that you identify to be of little value.
This exercise may even simply decrease your stress over certain activities by having
you recognize that the stress is simply not worth it. We will explore this in depth in
the next chapter.

4. **Insecurity** can be overwhelming. You may not feel that you measure up.

Thankfully, the Lord uses the ordinary to do the extraordinary. He has used many

average people to do miraculous things. He just as easily could have used those of

power. But if He had, His work would have not proven near as powerful. For example,

if God had used another Giant to defeat Goliath, no one would have batted an eye.

(Samuel 17:1-58). If you feel ordinary or just don't see yourself measuring up, rejoice

in what he is going to do with you!

5. **Entitlement** is the root of most, if not all, anger (Burns, 2016). We tend to believe

that if we do good things, we deserve good things. Unfortunately, there is no such

thing as universal fairness (Burns, 2016). Consider the lion and the lamb. The lion

eats the lamb to live. This is not fair to the lamb. However, if someone intervenes and

the lion is prohibited from eating the lamb, he dies hungry. This is not fair to the lion.

Remember there are *always* valid and opposing views that may be just as important as

yours. You do not have to understand others' points of view to accept that life is not

intended to be fair. Forego entitlement and you will be much less anxious as a result.

The book of Job is a powerful testament to this.

6. **Autonomy** is another false image that is senseless to chase. We never do anything

completely on our own. To begin, everything is through Him (Romans 11:36). Second,

everyone receives help in some form. It may be good fortune (or even just the lack of

horrible fortune), the right inspiration at the right God-given moment, being taught the

skills you learned, or simply an opportunity or good health, that many of us take for

granted. Lastly, if you place your value in doing His good work, and not upon building your pride, you will find value in everything you are a part of. Happiness and self-worth do not develop from worldly achievements. They will satisfy for only a short time before they ruin or become dated (Romans 12:2). However, life through Him will transform you everlasting (John 3:15).

7. **A fear of weakness** can stem from childhood or past experiences that we may wish we had handed better or from placing inaccurate values on ancillary characteristics, such as size. Do you have a history of abuse, trauma, or rejection that subconsciously leads you to feel inferior, imperfect, or weak? Did you hide things from friends that may have left you feeling "dirty" or "wrong"?. These experiences were out of your control and do not reflect upon you as a person. You did the best you could, given your circumstance. *It is what we do with ourselves after having faced those challenges that matter. It is what makes us strong.* Try to identify any associations that can free you from any negative and inaccurate self-perceptions.

8. **Fear of death** is common, which makes sense since survival is the most basic instinct. You may not realize you have this fear, because it does not always manifest as an obsession for fearing bodily harm. Fear of death may manifest as a fear of running out of time to get things done. When in fact you are fearful of running out of ultimate time. The best way to overcome this fear is, again, through the Lord. The promise of everlasting life easily overcomes this fear. Believing that you can receive such a miracle is where it gets tricky.

Chapter 4:

Overcoming

Perfectionism & Fear

A Journey of a Million

Miles, Begins

with One Step.

We discussed in the last chapter that perfectionism and fears are the cornerstones to many of our imbalanced identity priorities. Here we will work through specifically perfectionism and fear. Perfectionism is a difficult trap to get caught in. It becomes a crutch for us. But, when we let that perfectionism go, we can see what it is we are truly hiding underneath and that is the only way for us to more forward. You may be hiding behind impressive accolades, or a perfectly spotless house and it may help you to feel good for a while. But, if it becomes excessive, the question begs to be answered, "Why do I not feel worthy of acceptance even before those things are done?"

Fill out the below example with something that you find yourself caught in tedious tasks to finish perfectly or you feverishly feel (or felt) an excessive need to accomplish. There is an example for you first.

Stressful Task/Obsession: *Cleaning the house*

Resulting stress level: *7/10 sometimes a 10/10.*

What does the stress affect: *My happiness, my health. I get headaches from worrying. Stress and anxiety surrounding this affect my family's comfort with me & my mental health.*

What you miss out on as a result: *I miss out on time spent with family & peaceful moments.*

The value that maintaining this standard adds to my life: *Maybe a 4/10.*

Although cleaning is important, I still have not received any awards or compensation for it Furthermore, it never really accomplishes much, it always needs to be done

again the next day… or even hours later..

Interpretation: *The stress associated with maintaining an immaculate house does*

not outweigh the benefits & negatively affects more important things (family &

health). I need to find out why this is so excessively important to me. Am I covering up

another emotion? Am I using this as a way to prove my self worth to myself or others?

New Balanced Goals: *I will now only deep clean every other day and thus spend*

more time with family to decrease stress and improve happiness.

Now, it is your turn:

Stressful Task/Obsession:

Resulting stress level:

What the stress affects:

What you miss out on as a result:

The value that maintaining this standard adds to my life:

Interpretation:

New Balanced Goals:

This is the second tip I have for you in overcoming perfectionism. You can do

this very simply, even just in a moment without writing anything down. If you get

stuck in traps of stress, stop to evaluate whether what you are doing is worth the worry you put into it. Start by writing down your level of anxiety around performing a task, or multiple tasks, perfectly. Next, write out the value it added you're your life. If the anxiety was higher then the value either eliminate this task or begin to give it the credit it deserves. If the value was low, then make sure your time, energy, and stress associated with it next time are equally low. Keep in mind the things you could be doing in its place, that may add more value. This is not a suggestion to quit doing the necessary things in life, just one to find a healthier balance.

If you find yourself stuck in feelings of lack. Remind yourself of one of my favorite scriptures: *Look at the birds of the air; they do not sow or reap or store away in barns, and yet your heavenly Father feeds them. Are you not much more valuable than they? (Matthew 6:26).* I use this scripture to remind myself that if it is not done perfect, or I didn't get "enough" accomplished to remind myself that he will provide. I do not have to be pushing none stop. In fact, that is not even what He wants for me. He wants a purely beautiful life of abundance. That brings me to my second point in this chapter: **Fear is a liar**.

Just like anxiety and depression, fear will make us think irrational things. That which you feed, gets bigger. The more you feed your fear, the more real it will seem. Fear can even push you into believing that the ultimate price (ending your life) is better than living (Numbers 13-14 warns us of this). Search for what survivors of jumping from the Golden Gate Bridge thought as they fell. Not one of them felt at ease. Instead they felt immediate fear and regret. Depression, fear, and anxiety were lying to them, that death was better than life. Not until they felt it was too late could they see it. Don't let that be you, even if you aren't suicidal. Even if you are simply forfeiting days in your life by throwing every chance of enjoying them over a proverbial bridge. Don't let fear lie to you and let you believe that wasting days in bed or alone is better than getting out there in life. That is time you are killing that could be spent enjoying life and making this world a better place for not only you, but others. Believe that there is a happier place and know that is not only possible, but inevitable if you do not accept any other option.. It may take work, but it will be worth-it-work and you will find happiness.

Maybe fear, anxiety, and depression are telling you you are a bad person. I have news for you; they are lying to you again. No one is completely good or bad and therefore cannot be identified as such. What you have done in the past, does not label you, it educates you. Remind yourself of your good qualities and be proud that you are working on the rest. Everyone in this world is a work in progress. If we did not need to learn and grow, life would simply be too boring. Besides, I send you all the love and support in the world. But fortunately, friend it's not about you. Healthy IP's and mindsets tend to take the focus off of personal wants and desires and onto improving the world as a whole. That is a good thing. It is no coincidence that this is the Lord's' mission for us in doing His work. It is amazing how liberating and powerful this is. The pressure of life is lifted from your shoulders once this perspective shift takes hold. For example, instead of having an excessive need to be loved, emphasize loving others through acts of kindness. The love will return to you.

Instead of an unhealthy obsession for autonomy or personal success, focus your efforts on improving the community as a whole. You will not go unrewarded. You will thankfully give Him the glory as you obtain a sense of peace. Furthermore, being let down or disappointed becomes something of the past. When expectations are forgotten, everything in life becomes a bonus. The exception to this is, of course, are those who put themselves last to the point of it affecting their own health and well-being.

I know that it can be overwhelming diving deep into this. It can be even more overwhelming giving up some of the vices you have clenched to in the past. Slowing down your high achieving, showing your real and raw self and no longer   hiding behind large accolades, always giving too much of yourself to others searching for love in return,   or giving up always maintaining a super clean home, is terrifying... But, if you are feeling that sense of overwhelm, remind yourself that anything on this Earth that we are trying to accomplish without Him is ancillary and of no real worth. Everything that is His will, will be accomplished. If it doesn't happen, it was not a key aspect to His will and it too shall pass. And simply never forget the birds of the sky.

Lastly, look towards Eastern ideals that showcase how we need a balance of everything essential to keeping us healthy. Sometimes acknowledged as the Yin and the Yang. If we put too much energy into one thing, we cannot have that. You can always go back to these mental vices, but if you fully embrace wholehearted living, you won't want to. You'll find that you won't need them any longer. You will learn to live and love yourself for so many amazing reasons you may have not even thought possible. Furthermore, do not interpret this as needing to undervalue the parts of you

you find important. You are simply making yourself a part of something much greater.

Your purpose is not to be perfect, but to be a ray of light in every way that you can.

Chapter 5:

But, "THEY" made me mad!

Values are like fingerprints.

Nobody's are the same, &

We leave them all over

everything that we do.

-Elvis Presley

Believe it or not, others' actions are never the cause of our emotions (Leary, 2015). Instead of, *"They* made me mad!" you really mean, *"My Identity Priorities and thoughts* made me mad!" To understand what is really going on, break down the upsetting circumstance. For example, if you were told, "You're a jerk!" These words hurt, but only if they generate the right thoughts with significant meaning. If a stranger said this completely unprovoked, would you care? Instead of feeling mad, you may feel confused and think "Do they know me?" or "Are they mentally ill?" If you discover the person is mad because they said you cut them off in line, you might become defensive and upset.

The truth is that we get upset because our IP's are in jeopardy, not because of others words. In this example, associated IP's may be a need for approval, perfectionism, or a sense of entitlement. Your quest is to find which IP's fit the bill. An example of this process starts on the following page. IPs are not necessarily bad, it is simply when they negatively control our lives that they are unbalanced and therefore unhealthy.

How to Balance your IP's & Start to Feel Better:

With this exercise I want you to think about a specific time in your life when you have felt wronged by someone else. Then reflect upon that time while you answer the answers below. The first set includes examples and then the following one has blank spaces for you to fill in your personal experience.

1) Identify your initial thoughts and feelings:

In the example above of being called a jerk, you may initially feel inadequate, bad, or even rejected Remember that anger, sadness, and depression are not feelings. They are the result of our feelings (Burns, 2016). Therefore dive a little deeper and uncover how you feel by identifying what you think that means to you, or what you are afraid that says about you as a person.

2) Identify your IP's:

Refer back to the previous chapter to find what IP's you are using inaccurately. *The thoughts and feelings in our example are associated with a need for approval & perfectionism.*

3) Ask, "What does this mean?":

This is where things get real. Ask yourself, "If these IPs and/or thoughts were true, what would it mean?" In the following space keep repeating, "If this were true, what would it mean?" to each of your answers, until you find your root trigger. A root trigger is an actual reason for your emotions. It may be real or it may be one of the 11 Tricks. Either way, you will know it is the root trigger because it will particularly strike a chord with you. You may need to separate out each one if it is a complex issue.

*Using this example, you may ask yourself, "If they don't approve of me, what does it mean?" If it means nothing to you that a stranger doesn't like you, but you are still upset, then maybe you are not struggling with a need for approval. Is it a need for perfectionism? Ask yourself: "**What does it mean** if I mess up?" If the question* *bothers you, or you answer with one of the 11 Tricks, (such as, "I messed-up, as always") move onto Step 4.*

4) Challenge those negative thoughts and feelings:

Find how these thoughts are inaccurate. Refer back to Chapter 2 to help discover which tricks are being applied for you to maintain this unhealthy IP.

In our example, you may ask: Do I always mess up or is this All-Or-Nothing Thinking? (Hint: It is.) Now, disprove this negative thought. This one occurrence does not identify you as a person.

5) Identify what is (and is not) in your control: What is there that you can change about the event? What have you learned from it? What is something positive that can come of it? (More on this in Chapter 11: The Glass is Half Full). How can you make it better? What is out of your control?

If you messed up, remind yourself you are human and it happens. Apologize and know that it is okay to make mistakes. Make right what you can and move on. You could apologize, even if you didn't do anything wrong. Maybe you learned to be more careful in the future. Remember that we are all human, and humans make mistakes. Mistakes do not define us; it is what we do with these mistakes that defines us. If you are not able to make the other person happy, despite your efforts, realize that their actions are not within your control and accept that.

Balancing Your IPs

Describe a Bothersome Event:

1) Identify your initial thoughts, feelings, or emotions:

2) What IP(s) do they correlate with? (Review Chapter 4)

3) Ask, "If these IPs and/or thoughts are true, what would it mean about me?"

If the first were true, what would it mean to you, or about me?

->

What would that mean to you or about me??

->

What would that mean?

->

What would that mean?

->

If there is another negative thought, explore it here:

->

->

->

->

4) What tricks of anxiety or depression am I trying to use that I need to disprove?

5) What is in my control? How can I make this better? Or what can I learn?

Use the following pages to practice identifying and challenging your IPs with real life examples.

Building Healthy IPs

Negative Event #1:

1) List your initial thoughts, feelings, or emotions:

2) What IP(s) do they correlate with? (Review pages 24-25.)

3) Challenge your IPs: If these IPs and thoughts were true, what would it mean? (Use the following space to repeat, "What would this mean?" until you find your root trigger.)

Thoughts Or IPs Triggered:

Thought or IP #1:

Thought or IP #2:

Thought or IP #3:

If # 1 were true, what would this mean?

->

What would that mean?

->

What would that mean?

->

If # 2 were true, what would this mean?

->

What would that mean?

->

What would that mean?

->

If # 3 were true, what would this mean?

->

What would that mean?

->

What would that mean?

->

*Note that the questions read, "IF that were true…" *Reality is likely much different.*

Reality is what you are trying to discover.

4) Challenge these newly identified deeply rooted thoughts: How are they inaccurate?

Are they any of the 11 Tricks from Chapter 2?

5) What is in your control to change? Maybe there is some truth to your fears. If there

is something about yourself that you didn't do right, that is great you identified that and now know what bothers you. You now have the ability to begin to change it. What did you learn? What can you change to make the future better?

Lastly, as you work through different situations, try to notice trends about yourself. In the future these trends can be more easily identified and staying on a potentially negative path can be avoided faster.

Chapter 6:

Deceptive Rules & Limiting Beliefs

"IF I only had a heart"

The Wizard of Oz

"You've always had the Power my dear,

you just had to learn it for yourself."

--Glenda, The Good Witch

Another way to uncover the root of anxiety and depression is to identify your Deceptive Rules and Limiting Beliefs. This can be very in depth and you may have to put a lot of thought into these answers. But, I promise they will pay off. Start by, finishing the following sentence:

"I need _________, to be okay."

Examples include: I need *"to be successful", " to be loved/liked", or "to be not embarrassed or respected."*

The answers you find are Deceptive Rules. Deceptive Rules are those that you feel you have to achieve in order to be "enough" or a "good" person. They are deceptive because of that false placement on self worth. Keep in mind they are not overall bad, general rules to live by. For example, wanting to be successful or respected is not bad. But, very often when we want something so bad that it identifies our core value, we tend to have a subconscious fear that we are not it or do not deserve it. They then, paradoxically, prevent you from being your best. They falsely make you believe that what you are right now in this moment, is not enough. They tell you that you must "achieve" them to be complete. Unfortunately, without finding acceptance and love for yourself, these goals or desires will never bring you happiness.

Deceptive Rules tend to stem from comparisons of others that we erroneously tie to happiness. Such as having a lot of money, acceptance, or admiration from others. If someone who has these things is truly happy, their happiness will stem from something much more valuable than that: a humble appreciation and love for themselves. This is not conceded it is something that every person deserves. But I also want you to know that the shear appreciation of these goals or characteristics already prove that you embody them.

To demonstrate that truth, I would like to do a small experiment with you. Really, do this as you read this, don't skip it. Simply write down five people you look up to and then, next to their names, write the characteristics about them that you admire. Take some time and really think about what it is that you see in them that you like. This gives you insight to your personal goals or values. At the end of this chapter we will come back to this. Don't skip ahead to the end. Just set the list aside.

Next, got back to your Deceptive Rule and define the opposite of it to reveal your Limiting Belief. For example, if you have a Rule to be successful, the opposite is being unsuccessful. You may already perceive that you are a failure. If so, you discovered one of your Limiting Beliefs. Limiting Beliefs are something else that depression and anxiety use to trick us into having false ideas of ourselves. They *limit* us from achieving our goals, because they make us subconsciously *believe* we do not have what it takes, hence the term Limiting Beliefs.

Our beloved Tin Man from the Wizard of Oz saw that those around him had a heart. Therefore, he thought if he 'only had a heart', he too would be complete. His Deceptive Rule was that he had to have a heart. His Deceptive Belief led him to believe he was heartless (the opposite of having a heart). In fact, he was quite the opposite. He was full of love for everyone in his life, which is the true value in 'having a heart'. Once he could see that, he realized he was already complete.

Disprove Deceptive Rules and Limiting Beliefs the same way you disproved the 11 Tricks in Chapter 2. Start by assessing what Tricks you are applying to make them seem real. Next, evaluate the <u>real</u> definition of your Rule. All good and important qualities are a measure of many differing aspects. You can search online for qualities that relate to the Rule you subconsciously set for yourself and keep an open mind to other ideas or perceptions you may not have considered. The Tin Man had "The Great & Powerful" Oz to teach him what it truly means to have a heart. We have Google. A fair comparison, if you know the show.

For example, if your Subconscious Rule is: *"I need to be successful."* The Deceptive Belief is: *"I am unsuccessful."* First, evaluate what Tricks are being applied to call yourself unsuccessful. Then search for expanded definitions or qualities of what it means to be successful that already <u>do</u> apply to you. You may have only equated success to the amount of money you make. However, success can be based upon several different measures, such as helping others, finding happiness, raising kind children, or achieving a goal. We often do not give credit, where credit is do. Broaden the definitions of your goals, so you can see how great you already are.

Having the desire for success is the most important aspect of being successful. By having the desire, you already are, by virtue, a successful person. It takes time and work to achieve goals and there is no deadline written anywhere for that success to be achieved. You are on your time-line and the one God needs you to be on. Trust the process. Live and learn and be glad   Many Limiting Beliefs are this way, the simple desire to be them prove you *already are* them. For example, feeling guilty for the past and therefore *wishing* you were a good person is deceptive because you *already are* a good person (Burns, 2013). Bad people do not feel guilty for what they do. If you feel guilt, you are by virtue a good person. You are growing and evolving and that is a beautiful thing. In my opinion, even more virtuous and beautiful than someone who naturally became and did not have to overcome personal self growth to get there. Let the present and future define you, not the past.

Before we continue onto the second way you can reveal your Deceptive Rules and Limiting Beliefs, let's go back to that list of people you made. Pull the list back out and the next thing that I want you to do is cross out the names of those people. In place of their names, write down your own. Take that in for just a moment. Notice how that feels to be recognized to having those characteristics. First first step to becoming anything is *feeling* it to be true. Practice that feeling on a regular basis, until it becomes 100% natural. You would not be able to see and appreciate these characteristics in others if you did not already embody their essence. Everyone in this world is a constant work in progress. That is a beautiful thing. You may be on a different level with certain goals than you aspire to be, but that does not disqualify you from being on the spectrum.

Next, the following is a slightly different way to identify Deceptive Rules and Limiting Beliefs. If you feel comfortable with the first method, you may not need to do this slightly different one. However, if you feel there is something you are still not identifying, you can try this approach as well.

Step 1. Identify your Deceptive Rule by completing this sentence:

I am *not* okay or happy because ________________________________.

For example, "I am not okay because *others reject/make fun of me."* This means that you feel being accepted by others is necessary for happiness. It is the opposite of why you do not feel okay and is therefore your subconscious Deceptive Rule. Now let's evaluate this. Why should you care if people (maybe even those who are impolite to you), do not accept you? You shouldn't and you most likely are not actually concerned for that specifically. it is just what we naturally focus on. Most likely you deep down afraid of <u>why</u> they do not accept you, not the pure fact that they don't. Which is the purpose of the second step.

Step 2: Identify your Limiting Belief by answering this question: "What does it mean if someone does not 'measure up' to this rule?" We always have to ask "what that mean *about me* or why that identifies me as a person" to get down to the real issue.

Step 3: Next, objectively evaluate your answers and find any tricks of anxiety or depression or simply erroneous associations. For example, what does it mean TO THAT person (*as* a person) if they do not fit in? Maybe you answer, "It means they are unworthy or inferior." Being unworthy or inferior would thus be your Limiting Beliefs. A fear of being this is your actual true concern.

But, basing your self-worth on others opinion does not make much sense. How often have you received a bad grade on a paper because of someone else opinion of how they predict you would do? This is not typical, because others opinions do not predict your performance (unless you let it). Keeping this fear alive is applying

inaccurate Limiting Beliefs based upon Deceptive Rules.

Lastly, we need to find what really does make your the thing you afraid of not

being. If you are afraid of not being worthy or of being inferior, what identifies that?

Well, if we look towards our Father's teaching, we see that what makes us valuable, is

simply our being a child of God. Just as you are valuable to your parents, and your

children are to you. This is an unconditional rule for every person alive. But, having

your own set of values is not bad. I cannot set this for you. You must look within

yourself to identify what is of most value to you, and therefore most identifying as

your best form of self. For me, I set value in helping others, honesty, being genuine

with others and trying to maintain a selfless view. I certainly fall short of that. But,

when I know I am operating from a place of love, no one can make me feel guilt or

shame in myself, because I know my heart. That doesn't mean I am right, and I might

still need to adjust. It just means that I can let guilt and shame go and be able to move

forward if someone does not accept me, in person or on social media. The Lord

knows my heart, and that is enough for me. However, when I know I have fallen short

of that expectation of myself, I try to reset as quickly as possible. Hopefully better and

faster each time I fall.

Furthermore, being liked by others (The Deceptive Rule in our example)

would not make your Limiting Beliefs go away. Even if someone does approve of you,

that still does not mean you are someone you are comfortable with being. How many

times have you seen people conform to "fit in" and yet, still not be happy in their own skin. Be a person *you* are proud of. If others see it, then great. If not, that is okay. Just because someone else cannot appreciate your beauty or good qualities, it does not disqualify them.

While Limiting Beliefs are not factual, but they are often deeply rooted in highly influential beliefs that do affect your self-esteem (Manning & Ridgeway, 2016). To help you narrow it down further and help identify real root causes for discourse, here are four common types:

1) Feeling immoral or irresponsible

2) Feeling flawed or inadequate

3) Feeling unable to trust or relate to others

3) Feeling powerless, weak, or inferior

Do any of these resonate with you? They can be overcome. But first, we must find out more about them. Debilitating or mood altering emotions that may have been produced while reading about these four classes may cue you in for any inaccurate or magnified perceptions you could have about them. If you feel bothered, your heart races, or is anxiety provoked just thinking about any of these, try to identify why you feel this way. Look back over your previous entries or scan yourself for these types of thoughts and then practice identifying your Deceptive Rules and Limiting Beliefs. Which ones are triggers for your depression or anxiety?

Write them here:

Since Limiting Beliefs are inaccurate depictions, reassure yourself they are a result of false pretense and are at times, just another "trick" of anxiety and depression. Start by listing the facts. You may ask for help from a trusted friend or family member. Use the following pages to explore this.

Limiting Belief (LB) #1:

When did it start? Did someone else start it for you?

What tricks (from chapter 2) are being applied to keep this LB true?

Does it benefit you to continue to hold this belief?

Are there any built in defense mechanisms that you benefit from keeping it true? For example, do you get attention from others for continuing to hold this belief as a barrier in your life? Be honest with yourself.

What is a more accurate, healthier perception?

What facts support this new perception?

Repeat this exercise with as many LB's as you need.

Chapter 7

Squashing Negative Automatic Thoughts (NATs)

The only limits of tomorrow,

are our doubts from today.

-Franklin D. Rosevelt

Negative Automatic Thoughts (NATs) are inaccurate and negative thoughts that are so deeply ingrained, we automatically accept them and think them without deliberately doing so (Manning & Ridgeway, 2016). They impact feelings and are related to Limiting Beliefs. They tend to have some truth to them, but are equally misleading.

This exercise may take some time to develop. Spend the next few days being purposeful with your thoughts. As we become aware of our own NATs we will practice changing (or squashing) them. Before we practice though, I want to explore the difference of shame and guilt. Guilt is actually found to be protective in allowing us to keep our values straight. Experiencing it tends to keep us from repeating mistakes. Shame however, keeps us stuck in it. The most damage NATs are shame related. I discuss this with my team when discussing dietary changes. It is the most common reason why people tend to be stuck in unhealthy eating habits. Breaking free from it is essential and often over looked. Brene Brown is the leading mind in shame research. I highly recommend looking into her work if you are wanting a second book to read.

She states the research demonstrates that the easiest example of the difference between shame verses guilt is "I am bad" verses "I did something bad", respectively. Identifying yourself as the bad element is shame, whereas guilt is simply messing up and is not an identification of self. When you are trying to observe, and therefore not repeat, NATs, this is the biggest trend to observe and avoid. If you notice any shame statements, I recommend going back to your IPs and values and finding out what that really means to you and identifying your real fears. However, as a general rule, changing your NATs from shame based ones is a great start.

For example, change "I am a bad mom because I forgot to grab school snacks for the class" to, "I feel bad that I forgot the snacks." We have all been been, it does not identify you as a mom. No matter how much shame someone else may try to hand you. Now, write down some of the NATs you catch yourself thinking below:

NAT#1 (Example: I am a failure. I'm going to mess this up, as I always do.)

NAT#2

NAT#3

NAT#4

Now let's squash these annoying NATs by dissecting them out. For each one, answer the questions below. The first page provides an example in parentheses.

NAT #1: (Example: I*'m going to mess this up. I always do.*)

Evidence that it is true: (Example: *I have performed less than perfect at things like this before.*)

Evidence that it is false: (Example: *I always recover and learn from my mistakes. Each time I get a little better. Others often tell me that I do a good job.*)

New, balanced, and more accurate thought: (Example: *I may not perform exactly as I would like, but I always make it through. This time may be similar, but probably better, since I improve each time. Considering others praises, I am likely being too hard on myself.*)

NAT #2:

Evidence that the NAT is true:

Evidence that the NAT is false:

New, balanced, and more accurate thought:

NAT #3:

Evidence that the NAT is true:

Evidence that the NAT is false:

New, balanced, and more accurate thought:

NAT #4:

Evidence that the NAT is true:

Evidence that the NAT is false:

New, balanced, and more accurate thought:

NAT #5:

Evidence that the NAT is true:

Evidence that the NAT is false:

New, balanced, and more accurate thought:

Chapter 8:

Letting Go

(of Being Wronged)

Holding onto anger is like

drinking poison, but expecting

the other person to die.

-Budda

Let's focus on what happens when you feel wronged, disrespected, or cheated. Feelings of entitlement occur when we place our own emotions and beliefs onto the expectations of others. They are a leading, if not the leading cause, of anger. Therefore, it is likely that we can all benefit from some work in this area. First, we need to acknowledge that there is no universal rule for fairness. Rules such as, "I am polite, therefore others should be," are simply inaccurate and frustratingly impossible for any of us to control. People live by their own set of rules, just as you do (Burns, 2016).

Think of the lion and the lamb. The lion needs to eat the lamb to live. It is fair to the lion that he hunts the lamb for food. This is not fair to the lamb. But, if the lamb is taken from the lion, the lion dies of starvation. While this may be fair to the lamb, it is not fair to the lion (Burns, 2009). This truth can be applied to several instances in our day to day where overlapping needs in our society occur with societal interaction. We may not even be able to understand the others feelings or ideal, but that does not make others feelings unjust. I am certain that the lamb does not feel bad for the hungry lion, nor the lion for the lamb that escaped. Both have a right to live, but even though they may not be on the same team, we can see and accept that there is more than one side to a story. After considering this new perspective, can you accept there are different points of view, without having to understand each and every one?

How can you use this understanding to help you forgive others easier?

Provide some examples:

Now, you have to be able to forgive in order to set yourself free from the anger. With this new perspective, how can you change your perception of past events into positive ones? Could have that person been wronged in the past in a scenario that you are not aware of? Is it possible that their past made them hyper diligent of protecting their own feelings and fearful of being vulnerable to others?

Is there something, anything positive that came from the scenario? It may be as simple as being grateful for being shown what kind of person you do not want to be, so you never become it.

Life Pearl: *Being human ensures you will and have made mistakes. God forgives you each time, if you accept Him as your savior. No questions asked. Envision His forgiveness as receiving a "bucket of forgiveness" each time you falter. Your "forgiveness well" is certainly as full, as is any other human's. When someone wrongs you, imagine giving him or her one of your buckets, which were so graciously given to you.*

Lamenting on the past is not productive and it eats away at our happiness, which may be one reason forgiveness is so important to the Lord. Learn from the past. Then accept that what is done, is done. Write down what you are letting go of on a scrap piece of paper. Then throw it away, rip it up, or destroy it however you see fit. It only has as much power in your life, as you give it. Think about this: If you never again gave it thought, would it literally cease to exist in your world? Is it only alive because you give it life? If so, let it go. Quit breathing oxygen into a non-existent fire.

You must understand that only **you** can make yourself angry. Others cannot do it for you. I know there are scenarios where this is very difficult for any of us to understand. For example, the guy who cut you off in traffic is not who made you angry, you are. You can get mad and yell, "That idiot almost killed us, how ridiculous!" Or you can take a deep breath, become thankful, and think, "Thank goodness I was paying attention! That could have been bad!" The options for your reaction are the same in both situations. Your perception is what changes everything. You may feel that your "area" on the road was imposed upon. The moment you embrace the reality that nothing is promised to you, not your place on the road, not even tomorrow. Your priority changes from getting what you "deserve", to being thankful for what you were *given* (a wreck free afternoon). Your emotions go from anger to relief, and your reaction goes from destructive, to calm and productive.

If you are a mother or father, consider your child throwing a fit. It is not the child making you upset, it is most likely the thoughts you are telling yourself that lead to your anger. You may subconsciously be afraid that you are a bad parent. Do you live by a rule that children who are parented well don't act out? Change the dialect in your head. Sometimes children get cranky, just like anyone else. They may be in a developmental storm and therefore more irritable than normal. It does not mean you are a bad parent. It doesn't mean that they don't "respect" you. They may be upset about something else totally unrelated that they have not identified yet. It happens. When you feel others are "upsetting you". Ask yourself, "What does this mean about me?" Then, disprove those thoughts and recognize that it's not likely about you. If it is, fix what is in your control and move on.

Lastly, take note of the benefits of your positive reactions. Review past situations where you reacted negatively. Then brainstorm how you will change your perception. Consider more productive thoughts, IPs, perceptions, emotion, reactions, and the rewards that going from negative to positive will reward you with. Use the space below to journal about past or present times when others "made you" upset. An example is placed in italics.

Situation: *Cut off on the highway.*

Negative Reaction: *I could yell and get mad.*

Positive Reaction: *Or I could take a deep breath.*

Thoughts: *I was wronged!   verses I was fortunate.*

IPs Involved: *Entitlement verses Humbleness*

Perception: *I "own" a part of the road verses I do not own anything here.*

Priorities: *Getting what I "deserve" verses being happy to be alive and well.*

Emotions: *Anger verse Relief*

Reward/ Outcome: *No Reward for getting made verses finding something to be grateful and happy about.*

Situation:

Possible Negative Reaction:

Alternative Positive Reaction:

Potential Negative & Positive Thoughts:

IPs Involved:

Perception:

Priorities:

Emotions:

Reward/ Outcome for either situation:

It is also important to keep in mind that many times negative emotions, reactions, and/or thoughts can be the result of unrelated, or loosely related, frustrations. In the previous driving example, the anger may very well have been more deeply rooted in not wanting to go where the person was going. The negative reactions may have been a result of already being unhappy about going to work, for example. If applicable, identify any deeper reasoning for your negative emotions.

Situation:

Why you thought you were mad:

The real reason for your anger:

How do you overcome this anger?

How do you change your perception and stress?

Can you plan differently, or better balance your priorities (IPs)?

Reward/ Outcome:

Situation 2:

Why you thought you were mad:

The real reason for your anger:

How do you overcome this anger?

Can you change your stress, plan better, or better balance your IPs?

Journal what you have learned thus far in your journey. What are surprised to find out?

How will this benefit you in the future?

Chapter 9:

Be a Kid In a Candy Store

If you change the way

you look at things,

the things you look at change.

-Wayne Dyer

This chapter is as simple as it is difficult. We learned is Section 3, that only *you* have the power to make *you* mad. It's not others that make us mad, it's our thoughts and IPs that do it. Train yourself to always see the positive side of things. It is as much a practice, as it is an art. As Wayne Dyer famously put it, "If you change the way you look at things, the things you look at change." Has someone ever saw something in a completely different light as you, and their response blown you away? Maybe they were very wronged or even injured as a result of someone's negligence and still saw something positive from it. Maybe you couldn't perceive how they weren't upset. Even as difficult as it may be to comprehend, heir perception was likely not wrong, but either way more productive.

If you are to ever rid yourself of negative emotions, it is essential that you open your mind to alternative, more positive perspectives. As you travel through this journey, remind yourself of the power you can harness just by changing your perspective. You know how children see the smallest gifts as just amazing? It's almost ingrained in them to react with amazement and pleasure. Then life takes hold and that easy to please nature melts away. We begin to apply those inaccurate rules and IPs of what we think we deserve or what we can't let go of. We get the opportunity to go to a candy store as a treat, and instead of thinking "Yeah, candy!" we think, "There goes my waistline..."

Whatever you are in the habit of expecting and seeing, your brain will follow. If you are in the habit of finding the negative, that is what you will find. If you are of the mindset to expect positive things, *positive* is what you will see. Those Negative

Automatic Thoughts become second nature. But, they can be replaced with Positive Automatic Thoughts (PAT's). It only takes a good strong "PAT" to kill a "NAT" (meaning a "gnat"). All it takes to form a PAT is some thinking, creativity, and practice. Now, let's get back to being that kid in a candy store.

The next few pages list some common NATs. In the blank lines that follow, write out thoughts and emotions that could positively replace them. The first one is done for you. At the end, compare your answers with suggestions listed on page 72. Notice how many different ways you can change your thoughts, reactions, perspectives, and therefore life. This can be done by applying a very basic formula.

Basic formulas for doing this include either:

1) identifying how it was not as bad as it could have been,

2) finding the value in the outcome and being thankful for that value, or

3) re-balancing your IPs to healthy ones, or

4) learning how to look at change as an opportunity.

Your thoughts become your words, your words become your actions, your actions become your habit, your habit becomes your character, and your character becomes your destiny. -Chinese Proverbs

Even if these don't relate to your personal circumstances, fill them in. The key here is to practice your ability to look through the lenses of "rose colored glasses" so when an unexpected event occurs, you have the power to turn a NAT into a PAT. If you get stuck, you can refer to the following pages for examples.

Example:

Replace The NAT: *"That stupid driver cut me off!"*

With A PAT: *Thank goodness we didn't get into a wreck.*

1. Replace: *"I lost my job; now I will never catch up."* With:

____

2. Replace: *"I just blew that, as always."* With:

____

3. Replace: *"People never listen to me."* With:

____

4. Replace: *"Spilling my coffee proves today will suck."* With:

____

5. Replace:

  With:____

6. Replace: *"I have too much to do and it's stressful"* With:

____

7. Replace: *"I'm tired of waiting in line for my food!"* With:

____

8. Replace: *"I just wasted all that money!"* With:

____

9. Replace: *"This is the worst that could happen."* With:

____

Now fill in your own, actual NAT's that you have thought before and replace them with the glass half full, PAT's.

(Example answers to the previous page are on the next one.)

1. I am Replacing:

With: ____

2. I am Replacing:

With:____

3. I am Replacing:

With: ____

4. I am Replacing:

With: ____

5. I am Replacing:

With: ____

6. I am Replacing:

With: ____

Example ways to convert the NAT's from the original examples into PAT's, using the following 4 formulas:

      1) identifying how it was not as bad as it could have been,

      2) finding value in the outcome and being thankful for that value, or

      3) rebalancing your IPs to healthy ones, or

      4) learning how to look at change as an opportunity.

1. *"I am free to make my new destiny."* **This is an example of using formula 4, finding the opportunity.**

2. *"Glad I got that out of the way! I will learn from this and do better next time."* **This is an example of using formula 2, finding value.**

3. *To the world I may be one person, but to one person (i.e. wife, husband, mom..) I am the world.* **This is an example of balancing your IPs, formula 3.**

4. *Well, I got the bad karma out of the way early today, and at least it was on an old shirt!* **Formula 1.**

5. *My children may get less time with me, but they get more of with, with the time they have. Quality is better then poor quantity.* **Formula 4**

6. *I am fortunate to have so much worthwhile to fight for. When God gets me through this, I will have really taught my children how to be an overcomer.* **Formula 2 & 4.**

7. *This wait will make my food taste that much better!* **Formula 2.**

8. *That was a rude awakening. At least I know I won't let that happen again. It could have been worse.* **Formula 2 then 1.**

9. *The harder the journey, the more powerful the story. Or, The harder the setback, the stronger the comeback.* **Formula 4.**

<u>Bonus PATs:</u>

"I've overcome worse things. This too shall pass."

"The last time I thought something was horrible, it wasn't so bad. This time may very well be the same."

"If the devil is still after me, I must have something worth fighting for!"

"To err is human. We live, we learn. To quit learning and evolving would be the true misfortune."

Chapter 10:

Move the Mountain:

Overcoming Procrastination

& Motivational Paralysis

If you want to make an easy job seem hard, keep putting it off.

-Olin Miller

Procrastination and Motivational Paralysis are common symptoms of depression and anxiety. They keep us from doing what we know we should do, even when we feel bad about not doing it. They can even inhibit us from doing enjoyable things, such as spending time with family. It's not uncommon to have the motivation to go to work, but lack the drive to do much past that.

One simple solution is to evaluate and compare each activity. When you realize and measure the benefits of productive activities and the negative results of poor ones, deciding to take action becomes easier. When you see and record the gratification gained (or lost) from each action, it becomes easier to take action again in the future. This is one of two strategies for overcoming procrastination and Motivational Paralysis. View the following example of this first strategy. It evaluates exercising (the healthy, but daunting activity) verses watching TV (the easy, but not gratifying activity).

My 2 Options:

(Ambitious Activity Verses Comfort Zone Activity)

Exercising Vs. Watching TV

What reasons do I have to do each activity?

Exercise: 1. My Health. 2) My pride. 3) Feel better and improve my depression. 4) Time will pass either way, might as well make the most of it.

Watch TV: 1. I like to. 2) It's easy

How important are these reasons?

Exercise Reasons: All Are Very Important.

Reasons to Watch TV: Sometimes important, relaxing is good. But often, these reasons are not that important.

What reasons do I have to NOT do each activity?

Exercise: Just don't like it and I am tired.

Watch TV: 1. I know I will feel worse after. 2. It will make me even more unhealthy. 3. It's not a good example to set for my children. 3. It does not help me in achieving what I really want in life. It actually works against it.

How important are these reasons?

Exercise Reasons: Not very. I know I will have more energy if I actually do it.

Reasons to Watch TV: Very Important... Keeping this is pattern is literally negatively affecting my entire life.

After each activity was done: (You may need to reflect on past times if you didn't do both.)

Was Exercise Rewarding? Yes! I never regret a workout! I feel so empowered that I did this even when I didn't want to.

Was TV rewarding? At first it seemed to be. But I ended up feeling worse then when I started.

What Have I learned from this?

We do not get out of discomfort. I'll either feel bad for not working on myself and have to deal with those repercussions or I can benefit from putting in the work.

My 2 Options:

Ambitious Activity I Should Do, But Don't Really Want to:

Comfort Zone Activity I'd Rather, in the moment do:

What reasons do I have to do each activity?

Option 1:

Option 2:

How important are these reasons?

Option 1:

Option 2:

What reasons do I have *to not* do each activity?

Option 1:

Option 2:

How important are *these* reasons?

Option 1:

Option 2:

After each activity was done:

Was the activity rewarding?

Option 1:

Option 2:

What have I learned?

Technique II

This is the second technique for moving the mountain and ending

procrastination. Simply document the *anticipated* gratification of each activity before

doing it. Then, document the *actual* gratification you received from it (Burns, 2016).

Document a wide range of activities, from working, to spending time with family, to

doing chores, and especially doing "nothing", like watching TV. When you document

gratification in the following columns, do it as a percentage, where 100% is the most

gratifying and 0% is the least. Gratification can come from achievement, fun, or both.

Documenting this reveals that completing the most dreaded activities (i.e.

chores) give the most gratification, while those involving nothing (television

watching), leave us empty (Burns, 2016). Evaluating true gratification afterward

reflects this. When trends are revealed, it becomes easier to find motivation to do

more challenging activities in the future.

Activity	% Of Anticipated Gratification	% Of Actual Gratification Experienced
1.		
2.		
3.		
4.		
5.		
6.		
7.		
8.		
9.		
10.		

Chapter 10:

Closing Words &
Your Personal Tool Box

I am SO proud of you!! There are not many people who finish what they start. The pure fact that you made it here, proves that you are someone who will, if you haven't already, overcome your anxiety and depression! Treating anxiety and depression is complex. If you continue to struggle, do not give up. There are many approaches and tools available. This book is simply an introduction. Needing to explore and integrate several different approaches before finding remission is common. However, rest assured that while most feel helpless, no one is, everyone is within hope and you will continually improve. It is additionally important to realize that medications are often necessary. Imbalanced neurotransmitters can lead to symptoms largely out of personal control. Additionally, chronic stress can physically change our brains making it even more challenging to find remission. If recommended by your healthcare provider, medication can be a great intervention to help calm the waters (so to speak), and allow you to think more clearly.

Anxiety and depression are challenging aliments. Expecting anyone to just "get over it" is as nonsensical as expecting a diabetic to just start using their own insulin correctly. But, no matter how difficult is may be to finally overcome your anxiety or depression, achieving a sound mind can be the most rewarding feat you will experience. Lastly, remember that anxiety and depression are often lifelong challenges. You may find yourself constantly practicing and reviewing your strategies and toolbox (which is found on the next page). This is not to be of discouragement. Everyone is a work in progress. It is when we stop growing and learning that we should worry. Lastly, I would love to hear your progress and breakthroughs. Please, feel free to reach out to me at DrLaurenAPRN@gmail.com. I will be looking forward

to hearing from you.

Many Blessings,

Lauren.

Personal Toolbox

Use the following pages as a quick reference for the strategies you found most helpful.

Think about these as your "Ah-ha!" moments and write them here. These pages are

like a toolbox to store and quickly reference strategies and thoughts that have been the

most helpful to you. When you feel lost or are having a rough time dealing with

depression or anxiety, turn back to these pages.

References and Continued Learning

Barsade, Sigal G. "The Ripple Effect: Emotional Contagion and Its Influence on Group Behavior.55 Administrative Science Quarterly, vol. 47, no. 4, Dec. 2002, pp.644-675 EBSCOhost, doi: 10.2307/3094912

Bernbau, H., Fujita, F., & Pfennig, J. (1995). Consistency, specificity, and correlates of negative emotions. Journal of Personality and Social Psychology, 68(2), 342–352. https://doi.org/10.1037/0022-3514.68.2.342

Bhargava, H. (2016). Meditate your way to better health. Retrieved from: https://www.medscape.com/ viewarticle/870131

Brauser, D. (2017). Even mildly insufficient sleep associated with increased risk for depression, anxiety, symptoms. Retrieved from: https:// www.medscape.com/viewarticle/879098

Burns, D. (2009). Feeling good: The new mood therapy. HarperCollins Publishers. New York, NY Grenny, J., Patterson, K., Maxfield, D., McMillan, R., Switzler, A. (2014). Influencer: The science of leading change.

Brown, Brene, (2018). Daring greatly. Audiobook. Retrieved from Audible.

de Graaf, L. E., Roelofs, J., & Huibers, M. J. H. (2009). Measuring dysfunctional attitudes in the general population: The Dysfunctional Attitude Scale (form A) revised. Cognitive Therapy and Research, 33(4), 345–355. https://doi.org/10.1007/s10608–009–9229–y

Hoftnann, S., Asnaani, Vonk, I., Sawyer, A., Fang, A. (2013). The efficacy of Cognitive behavioral therapy: A review of meta-analyses. US National

Library of Medicine National Institutes of Health.

Retrieved from: https://www.ncbi.nlin.nih.gov/pinc/ articles/PMC3584580

Knaus, W. J. (2014). The cognitive behavioral workbook for anxiety: A step-by-step program. 2nd Ed. Raincoast Books. Oakland, CA.

Leary M. R. (2015). Emotional responses to interpersonal rejection. Dialogues in clinical neuroscience, 17(4), 435–441. https://doi.org/10.31887/DCNS.2015.17.4/mleary

Manning, J & Ridgeway, N. (2016). CBT Work Sheets. West Suffolk CBT Service Ltd.

MacReady, N. (2019). Emerging health concern: Additives causing harm in children. Retrieved from: https ://www.medscape. org/viewardcle/900593

Marsh, R. (2018). Ray of Hope, Women's Conference. Comanche, OK. Referencing: White, D. (2017). Vertical Living.

New International Version: Quest Study Bible. (2003). Zondervan. Grand Rapid, MI.

Ostell, A., Oakland, S., (2001). Absolutist thinking and health. Wiley Online Libraiy: British Journal of Medical Psychology. Vol 72 (2). https://doi.org/ 10.1348/000711299159989

Potter-Efron, R. (2007). Rage: A step-by-step guide of overcoming explosive anger. Raincoast Books. Oklaland, CA.

Piedmont Healthcare. (2018). How exercise helps balance hormones. Retrieved from: piedmonthealthcare. org

Rnic, K. Dozois, D., Martin, R. (2016). Cognitive distortions, humor styles, and depression. Vol 12 https://doi.org/10.5964/ejop.vl2i3.1118

Smalley & Cunnmghain. (2009). From anger to intimacy: How forgiveness can transform your marriage. Regal Books. Grand Rapids, MI.

Quines, C., Rosa, S., Rocha, D., Gai, B., Bortolatto, C., Duarte, M. Noguiers, M. (2014). Monosodium glutainate, a food additive, induces depressive like and anxiogenic-like behaviors in young rats. NCHI. 107(27-31. doi: 10.1016/j.lfs.2014.04.032.

Starosahl, K., Robinson, P. (2017) The Mindfulness & acceptance workbook for depression. 2nd Ed.

Raincoast Books. Oakland, CA.